Succe[ss]

A Practice Workbook on Reading for Facts

If you turn to page 8 you can join the crazy B team on their dream boat!

And there's lots more inside! ➡

Author Dr Alan Peacock
Educational Consultant Dr Roger Merry
Illustrator Dave Parker

Hatchet's helpful hints

We're very keen on finding out things, Gus and I, so here are a few ideas to help you....

Think of all the times you need to find facts for yourself. You often have to find facts at school. And there are lots of times when you have to find out things at home.

From a book

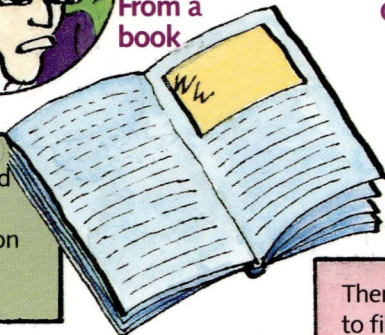

You can find out more about this on page 18.

On a form

SIGN HERE ....

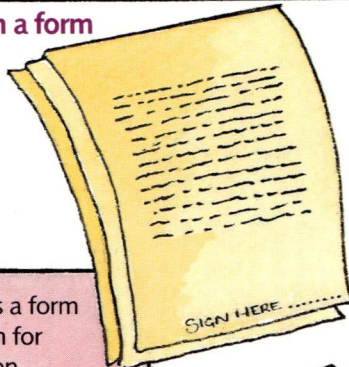

There's a form to fill in for Skulk on page 7!

From instructions

D.I.Y. KIT
D. I. Y.

You'll find examples on page 10.

You'll find examples on page 16.

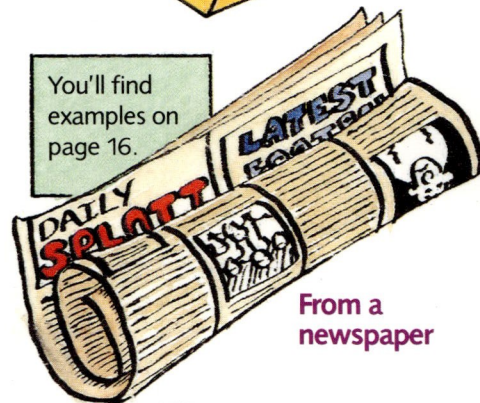

DAILY SPLATT
LATEST

From a newspaper

From diagrams

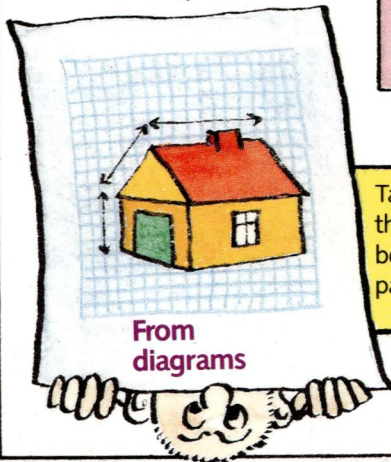

Take a look at the dream boat on page 8.

Splotto
CARD GAME

From rules

Try playing Tricia's game on pages 11 and 12.

What I always say is:

1. Ask yourself 'What am I looking for?'
2. If you want to know what's in a book, look at the contents page first.
3. Read things carefully.
4. If you don't know what something means, ask someone, or look it up.
5. Don't just rely on words: diagrams, maps and pictures are also there to help you.

REFERENCE BOOK

Gargoyle's out of order

Typical Gargoyle! He's torn half the labels off the slugfood tin! I can't work out these instructions.

Can you help Skulk with the instructions for Sluggigrub? Number the torn pieces of paper in the correct order.

LEVEL IT OFF WITH A KNIFE

POUR SLUGGIGRUB INTO FEEDING

A SPOONFUL OF SLUGGIGRUB

STIR IT UNTIL FROTHY AN

DD TO A BUCKET OF WATER

SLUGGIGRUB

2. 1.

4. 3.

5.

BEST BEFORE JUNE 1964

SPECIAL OFFER

Collect 2000 labels from 'Sluggigrub' and we'll send you a free slughouse kit

Remember: Getting things in the right order is important in recipes or science or history.

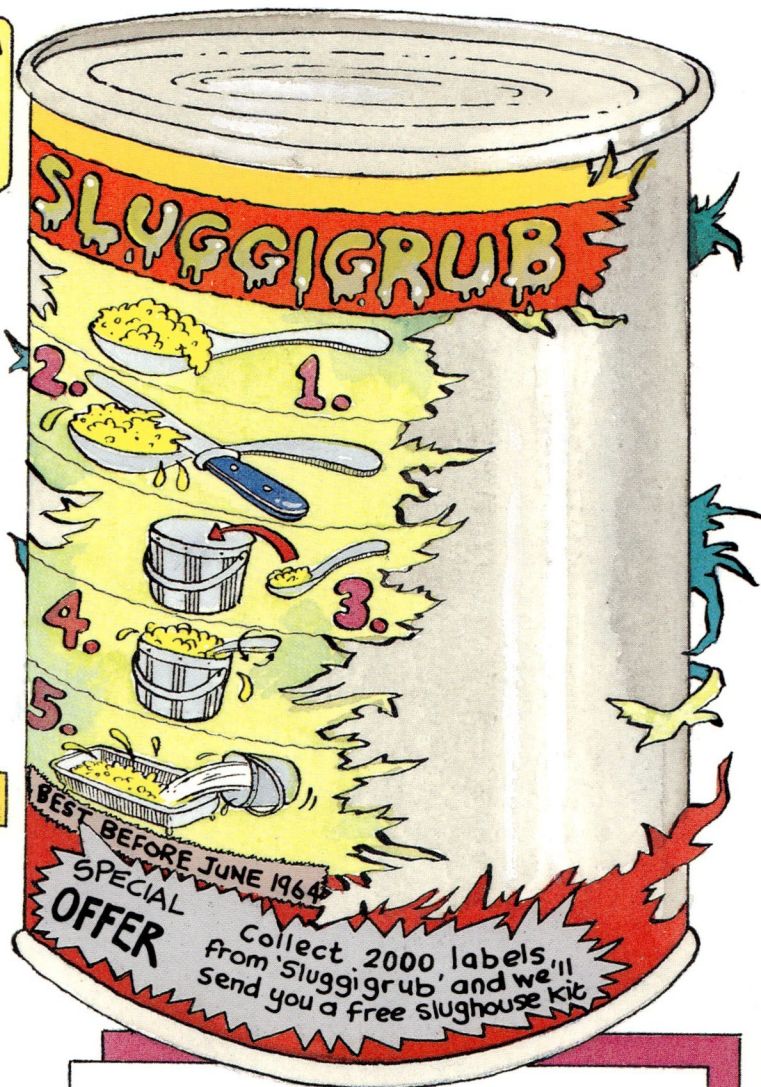

Make your own puzzle for a friend to try! Find some instructions and copy them out on pieces of paper. Mix up the instructions. See if your friend can get them in the right order.

Notes for zoo robbers

Hatchet's found a book on zoo robbing. We need some handy notes when we're robbing the zoo.

Hatchet didn't want to copy the whole book. So he decided to underline all the important words and use them for his notes.

Elephant catching

Equipment: jam jar, binoculars, tweezers

If you decide that you want to catch an elephant, first take a pair of binoculars. Look at the elephant through the binoculars the wrong way round. The reason for doing this is to make it look very small. Now all you have to do is pick the elephant up with the tweezers and drop it into your jam jar.

Hatchet's notes

Elephant catching

Equipment: jam jar, binoculars, tweezers. Take binoculars. Look at elephant wrong way round to make it look small. Pick elephant up with tweezers — drop into jam jar.

Can you help Hatchet make his notes? We've done the first one for you.

4

Underline all the important words (try not to underline more than half). Then write your notes on a small piece of paper.

Hippo stealing

Equipment: rope, four skateboards, candy floss

If it's a hippo you want to steal, first take a large stick of candy floss (this is the hippo's favourite food). Then dangle the stick of candy floss as near as possible to the hippo's nose. Hippos are very greedy, so it will eat the candy floss straight away. Now all you do is put the rope round its neck and push its feet onto the four skateboards. You can now pull it quickly out of the zoo.

Baby python picking

Equipment: sock, pencil

First of all, you need to catch your baby python. As soon as you have caught the python put a nice, woolly sock over its head. You do this to blindfold it. To make it easier to carry the python away, wrap it carefully round a large pencil and place it in your top pocket.

Try to pick out important words whenever you make your own notes.

5

Snailympics form filling

Our snails are training hard for the Snailympics. We're entering them for six different events.

The snails are looking super fit.

Can you help Skulk and Gargoyle fill in the entry form?

23

6

1992 SNAILYMPIC GAMES

Entry form

Please put a tick next to the events for which you are entering snails.

Bobbing		Diving		Ski-ing	
Boxing		Hopping		Sliding	
Canoeing		Jumping		Spinning	
Climbing		Kicking		Swimming	
Crawling		Riding		Throwing	
Creeping		Rowing		Trailing	
Curling		Running		Vaulting	
Dancing		Skating		Walking	

Type of diet required for competing snails: *(please tick one only)*

Lettuce ☐   Chips ☐   Beefburgers ☐   Bluebottles ☐

The snails are/are not amateurs.
The snails have/have not taken
shell building drugs.
(cross out as applicable)

No. of events entered: ☐

Entry fee – £10 per event: £

(fill in the total in the box)

Name: ....

Address: ....

....

.... Post code: ....

All entry forms should be sent to The
Secretary, Snailympic Village, by 1st January
1992.

Remember: it's
important to fill in
forms without
making mistakes.
Read the whole
form carefully
before you start to
fill it in.

*Skulk and
Gargoyle live at
Ghoul End
Guest House.
Can you make
up a ghoulish
address for
them?*

7

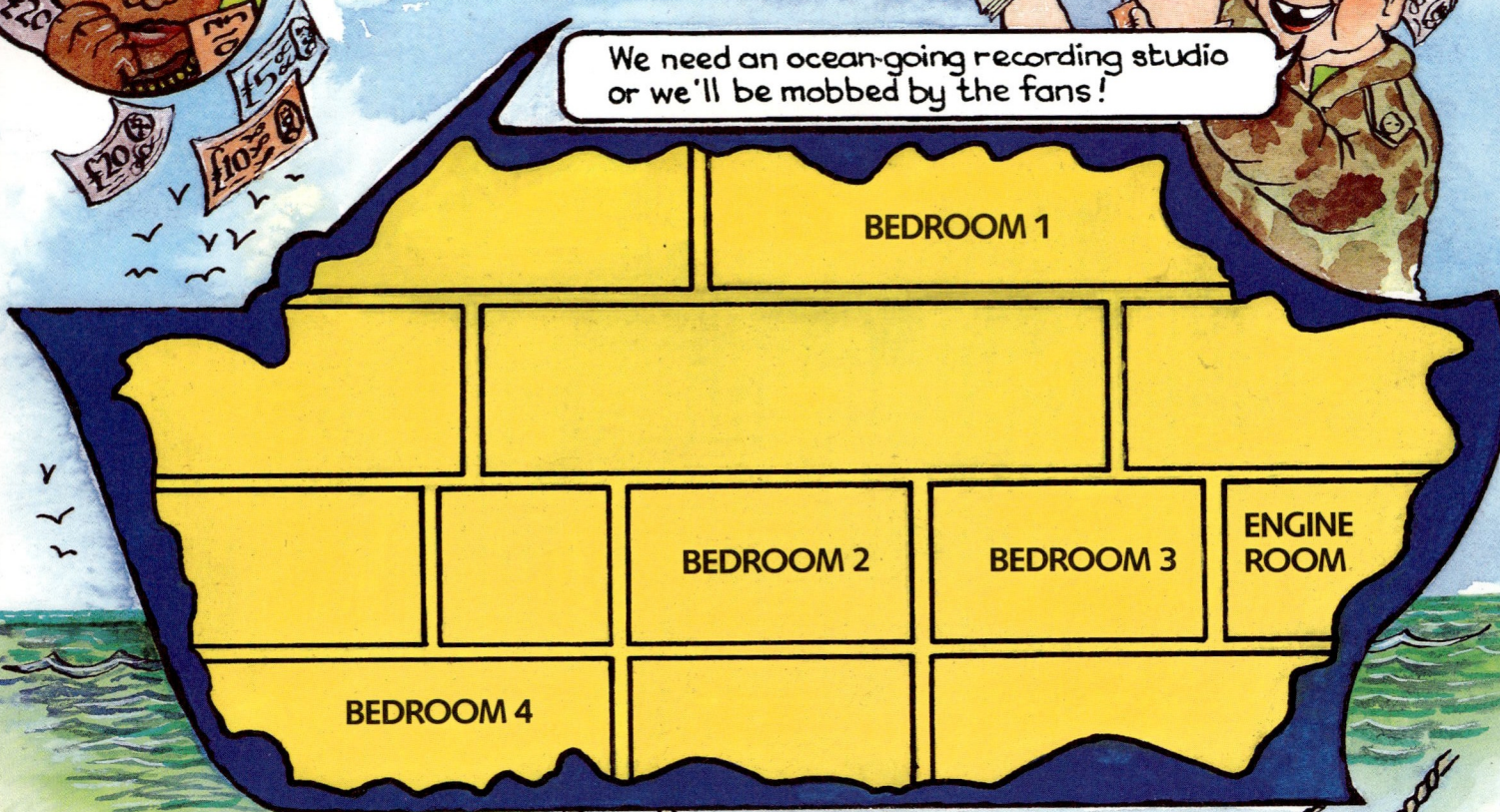

Can you help the B team design their dream boat?

It will need:

* 4 bedrooms
* recording studio ✓
* cook's hammock room
* kitchen
* pool
* disco
* restaurant
* sun lounge
* gymnasium

The problem is ...

Mr. U: The recording studio must be the biggest room.....

Cannibal: and it must be in front of the disco.....

Cannibal: The sun lounge must be at the top of the ship.

Myrtle: Put my bedroom next to the kitchen!

Myrtle: My bedroom must be quiet: as far away as possible from the disco.

Feetman: The restaurant must be above the sea - or we'll all be sick.

Mr. U: I'd like the bedroom above the gym.

*Can you fill in where the rooms will go on the plan? Some of the rooms can go in different parts of the boat. Decide what **you** think is the best place for each room.*

HINT: Use a pencil, you may have to change things as you go along.

Myrtle: We forgot the swimming pool. Where do _you_ think would be the best place?

9

Sorting out the slughouse

Gargoyle's tipped everything out of this kit and lost the labels. I'll just have to read these instructions!

Can you sort out the slughouse? Read the instructions first, then letter the parts (A to F) correctly.

SLUGHOUSE KIT

SLUGHOUSE KIT

Instructions for assembly

★ Open the collapsible frame (A) out and join together all corners.

★ Check that slugflap (B) is flapping freely.

★ Fit slugflap into hole in door (C)

★ Slot the door into place in the frame.

★ Place sheets of 'slimyglass' (D) into collapsible frame.

★ Connect slug warmer (E) to mains and place in slughouse.

★ Stand feeding trough (F) over slugwarmer for lovely warm slugfood.

Oh dear, I'm in trouble again! Can you help me assemble the slughouse?

If you're making something from a kit, it's important to read the instructions carefully to understand how the parts fit together.

Playing by the rules

I can't wait for the holidays! I've made up this board game – do you want to try it? You'd better read the rules first!

You're flying to Australia on holiday. But lots of things can happen to you on the way. You might not even get there! You may get one week of holiday – or lots more! Play the Holiday Game to find out!

Before you play

★ As many people as you like can play.

★ You need dice and a coloured counter each (that's your plane).

★ Each player starts with six HOLIDAY VOUCHERS. (Yippee!)

Make lots of vouchers like these: one voucher = one week's holiday. For each player you need six vouchers to play with and seven extra in the bank.

Voucher

Voucher *Voucher* *Voucher*

How to play

★ Start at Manchester Airport.

★ If you land on a *yellow square*, pick up one or two vouchers from the bank.

★ If you land on a *red square*, you *lose* vouchers. These go back to the bank. It tells you how many on the square.

★ If you use up all your vouchers, you're out of the game.

★ The player who reaches Australia first wins **two** extra vouchers. When all the players have reached Australia THE WINNER is the one with the most vouchers. (Bet it's me!)

You can play on your own.

11

START HERE

MANCHESTER AIRPORT

Lose 1

fog

Forgot money
Lose 3

WIN 2

Forgot suitcase
Lose 1

Lost passport
Lose 4

Bad weather
Lose 2

FINISH HERE

AUSTRALIA

	Waiting to land Lose 1
Win 2	
	Stuck in toilet Lose 1
Win 1	

Please keep this door closed

Sick Lose 1

	No food Lose 2
Win 2	
Win 1	

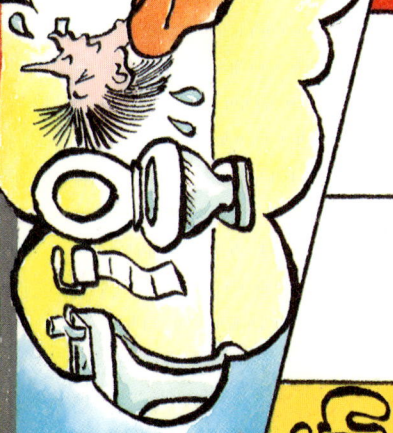

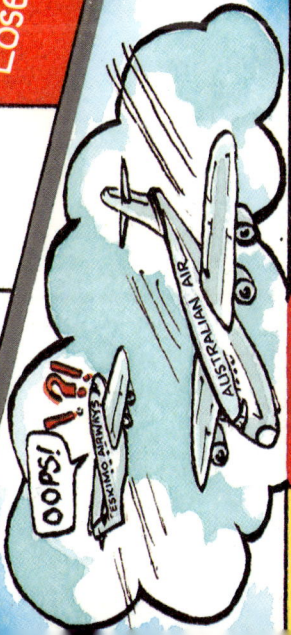

OOPS! !?!

AUSTRALIAN AIR

ESKIMO AIRWAYS

Win 2	
	Wrong plane Lose 2
Win 1	

Now you can play the Holiday Game, try playing with a friend! Can you explain the rules to them?

Follow Maud's map

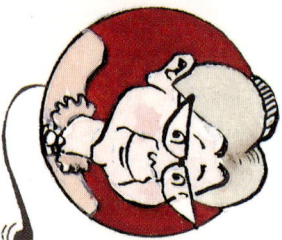

Elsie wants to visit her boyfriend Bert, so I've given her a map and some directions.

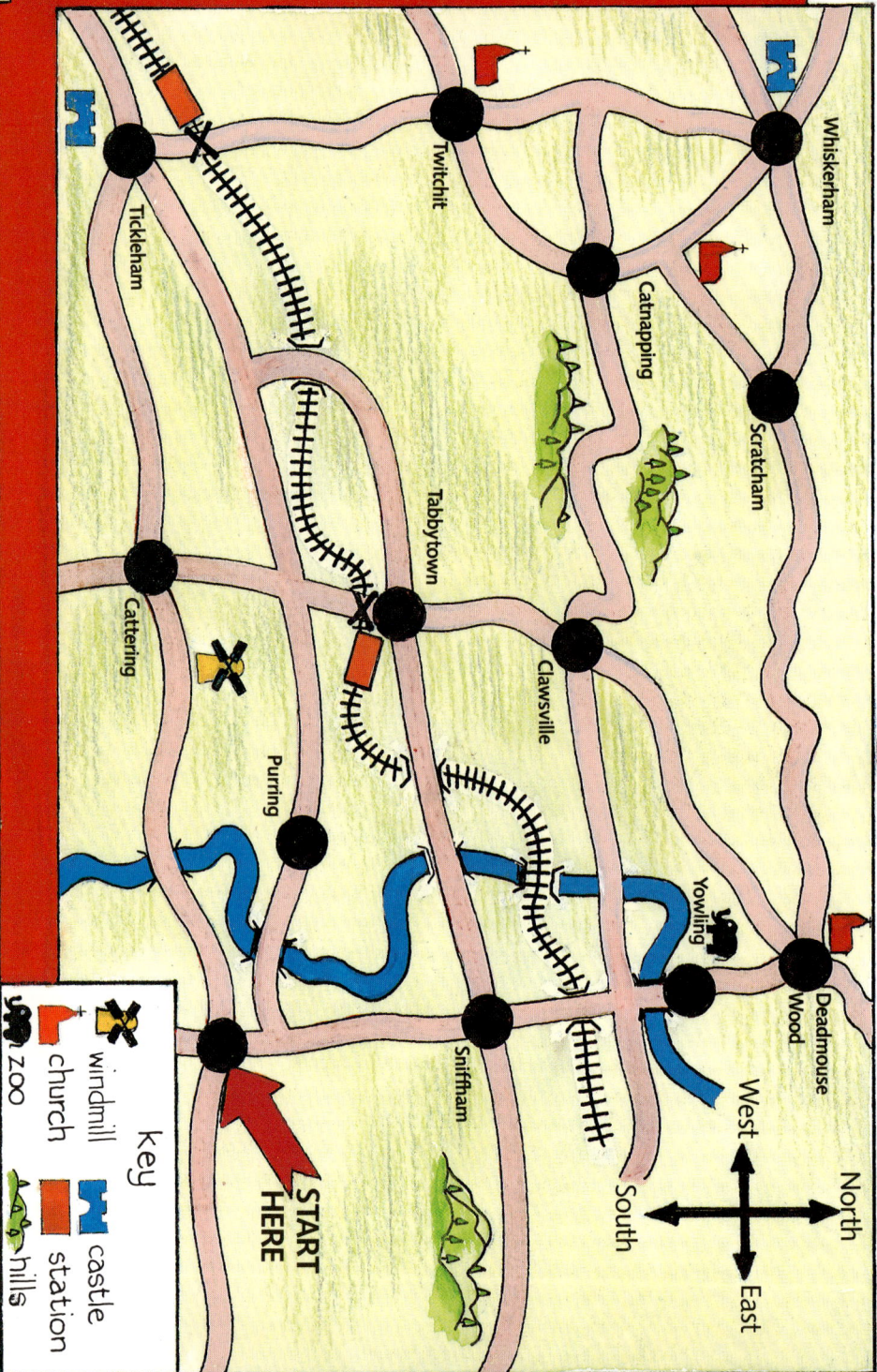

Whiskerham

Twitchit

Catnapping

Scratcham

Tickleham

Tabbytown

Clawsville

Cattering

Purring

Yowling

Deadmouse Wood

Sniffham

START HERE

key

windmill
church
zoo
castle
station
hills

North
West — East
South

Trace Elsie's route and tick all the places which she visited on her way to Bert's bungalow.

Catnapping

Purring

Tickleham

Cattering

Scratcham

Twitchit

Clawsville

Sniffham

Tabbytown

Yowling

Whiskerham

Deadmouse Wood

How to get to Bert's bungalow
(visiting some of Ronald's favourite villages on the way)

Set off west, across the river.
Go past the windmill, then turn right.
Go straight on at the first crossroads.
Turn right past the railway station.
Cross the river and turn north.
Keep straight on past the zoo,
then turn first left.
At the next village, head for the hills.
Take the third exit at the roundabout.
Fork left at the church.
Bert's bungalow is in the next village.

Which village does Bert live in?

....

Elsie is taking Bert back for tea at the cottage. Bert wants to visit the zoo on the way.

Can you trace Elsie's quickest way back on the map? Can you write instructions for Elsie?
You can use the names of the villages.
(You'll need some paper and a pen.)

Finding the right holiday

The Splott Street kids are fed up of beach holidays and want something different.

P.S. I think I'll go and learn about philosophy.

PLATO

Paul Just give me a quiet river and a fishing rod.

Reshma I fancy mountaineering, but not too far from home.

Tricia I want to learn to fly a plane.

Lee I just want to meet people and make new friends.

Weedy My mum says I should learn weightlifting, and eat more food.

Ali I want lots of excitement, nightlife too, but I hate sunbathing.

Lisa Anywhere to get away from this lot – as long as it's quiet!

What type of holiday should they look for? Write down the numbers they should ring:

TRICIA	
WENDY	
PAUL	
LISA	
LEE	
RESHMA	
SID	
ALI	
YOU	

What number would you ring? Now try finding interesting holidays in a real newspaper!

SPLOTT STREET ECHO   29.1.93

Holiday Guide

Overseas

CLUB 19 – make friends and you'll never be lonely. 11223

ENDLESS SAND, sparkling sea, marvellous hotels, go on, be tempted . . . phone 10101

UP THE AMAZON! Paddle your own canoe, get away from everybody. 44444

FLY TO FLORIDA and see Disneyworld. Call 60043

NIGHTLIFE, WEATHER, WONDERFUL BEACHES, everything you could want. 21945

ICELAND, for volcanoes, hurricanes and the nightlife of Reykjavik. Tel. 76021

TRY THE ALPS of France and Italy for your next climbing holiday. Tel. 20202

Special Interest

HEALTHLAND for good food, rest, all kinds of body building – phone 99999

FREE AS A BIRD with our cheap lessons. All planes regularly tested. 98765

SUMMER SCHOOL for Stimulating philosophers for super brains. surroundings. 62568

ROY'S REST HOME for cuddly cats and their proud owners. Truly a holiday with a difference. 70734

Activity holidays in the UK

THE WELSH MOUNTAINS – good to reach, easy rugged. Phone 12345 campsites.

HANG GLIDING in only 3 days! As easy as falling off a cliff. 54321

TROUT FISHING in peaceful surroundings. Call us on 82461

THE GENIUS' GUIDE TO USING INFORMATION BOOKS

By Sid Genius

I've lent this book to Weedy to help him find things in books ...

... I had to mark all the difficult words for him, of course!

The title of the book is on the front cover, so read this first to see if the book is about the subject you are interested in. Turn to the contents page at the front of the book, which lists the main sections of the book: these are called chapters.

Sometimes there will be different headings in the chapter. These will help you find what you want to know more quickly. Smaller sections, each with a few sentences, are called paragraphs. This is the end of the second paragraph of The Genius' Guide.

If you have trouble finding what you want, try the index at the back, which lists the contents in alphabetical order.

Weedy looked up all the difficult words in a dictionary, but then he got them mixed up.

Can you match the right words from The Genius' Guide to Weedy's list of meanings? Write the answers here.

subject

contents

paragraph

index

headings

title

chapters

This is the best use of the contents of this book, Sid!

DICTIONARY

A What the book is about

....

B A list of chapters in a book

....

C A section made up of several sentences

....

D The alphabetical list at the end of a book

....

E The main sections in a book

....

F These come at the start of chapters, or in chapters to help you find what you want to know

....

G The name of a book

....

Gus has built a T.V. satellite dish from a dustbin lid, but we can only get three strange channels on it.

Let's see, are there any sport or any wildlife programmes?

I prefer crimes and cookery myself.

Which programmes should they watch?

Can you fill in Gus and Hatchet's lists?

Are there any times when Gus and Hatchet both want to watch T.V.? Yes/No
What programmes will clash? ....

Gus' list of things to watch: Sports and wildlife

PROGRAMME	TIME	Start	Finish

Hatchet's list of things to watch: Crimes and cookery

PROGRAMME	TIME	Start	Finish

ROCKALL T.V.
'Rockin' the Atlantic'

4.00 Floyd on Rockall – 101 ways to cook seaweed

4.30 No neighbours

5.00 Rockallympic Games

9.00 Shark-eating seagulls of Rockall

9.30 Close

WORRALOADA T.V.
'The voice of the outback'

12.00 Kangaroo racing – Worraloada Grand National

1.00 Inspector Wogga investigates

1.45 Worraloada news

2.00 Ten ways to cook a boomerang

2.30 Close

SWITCHITOVA T.V.
'Switchitova every night'

8.00 Dracula and the detective

9.30 Sandwich making for beginners

9.45 Endangered species: the two toed tree bat

10.00 Storytime: The lion, the switch and the wardrobe

11.00 Close

Answer page

Page 3

Correct order

1. (Take) a spoonful of Sluggigrub
2. Level it off with a knife
3. (Add) to a bucket of water
4. Stir it until frothy (and yucky)
5. Pour Sluggigrub into feeding (trough)

Pages 4-5

These are the notes we made. Yours might be similar.

Hippo stealing

Equipment: rope; four skateboards; candy floss of zoo.

Take candy floss – dangle near hippo's nose. It will eat candy floss. Put rope round its neck. Push feet onto skateboards. Pull quickly out of zoo.

Baby python picking

Equipment: sock; pencil

Catch python. Put sock over its head to blindfold it. Wrap it round pencil. Place in top pocket.

Pages 6-7

Ticked activities should be: Boxing, Canoeing, Climbing, Ski-ing, Swimming, Vaulting.

The entry fee is £60.

Pages 8-9

Several possible solutions – here is one:

Page 10

A (Collapsible frame)
B (Slugflap)
C (Door)
D (Slimyglass)
E (Slugwarmer)
F (Feeding trough)

Pages 14-15

Elsie visited: Catnapping, Cattering, Clawsville, Sniffham, Deadmouse Wood, Tabbytown, Yowling.

Bert lives in Whiskerham

The quickest way home (visiting the zoo on the way) is via Scratcham, Deadmouse Wood, Yowling and Sniffham.

Pages 16-17

They should ring the following numbers:

Tricia	98765	Reshma	12345
Sid	62568	Weedy	99999
Lee	76021	Ali	11223
Paul	82461	Lisa	44444

Pages 18-19

A subject B contents C paragraph D index
E chapters F headings G title

Pages 20-21

GUS' PROGRAMMES

	TIME	
	Start	Finish
Kangaroo racing	12.00	1.00
Rockallympic Games	5.00	9.00
Shark-eating seagulls	9.00	9.30
Endangered species	9.45	10.00

HATCHET'S PROGRAMMES

	TIME	
	Start	Finish
Inspector Wogga	1.00	1.45
Ten ways to cook a boomerang	2.00	2.30
Floyd on Rockall	4.00	4.30
Dracula and the detective	8.00	9.30
Sandwich making	9.30	9.45

Rockallympic Games and Shark-eating seagulls will clash with Dracula and the detective.

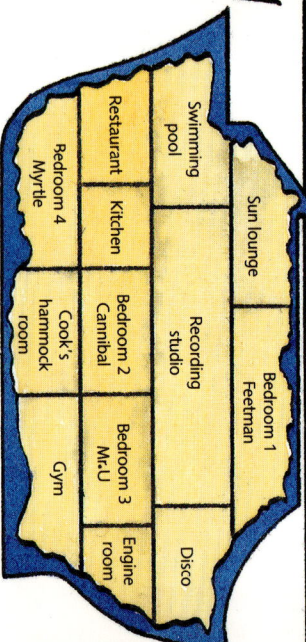

Check your reading powers!

1. On which pages can you find these things?

	Page
Notes on hippo stealing	....
A form to fill in	....
A game to be played	....
A book about books	....

2. Here are some cards with the names of activities in this book. Mark each card with the correct letter to show which box it goes in.

A	Completing a diagram
B	Finding information from a newspaper
C	Putting things in order
D	Using information to make lists
E	Following instructions
F	Following directions

1. Gargoyle's out of order ☐

2. Design a dream boat ☐

3. Sorting out the slughouse ☐

4. Follow Maud's map ☐

5. Finding the right holiday ☐

6. Gus' satellite television ☐

3. Write the name of the activity you choose in each of these sentences:

I thought .... was the most enjoyable.

I thought .... was the most difficult.

I thought .... was the one I did best.

HOW THIS BOOK *works*

Sit down together to look at the book. Go through the activity on page 2 and then begin any other activity just to get the feel of it. Look at the other pages too — there's lots of **FUN**.

Once started, **PRAISE** your child's first efforts, then just let them work independently. One of the great things about *SUCCESS!* is that you don't have to be there all the time. Do make sure, though, that you're around if your child needs your help or wants to show you what they've done.

HOW TO CHECK YOUR CHILD'S READING POWERS

When most of the activities are finished, suggest your child tries page 23. How well did your child do in answering the second set of questions? These test your child's **understanding** of the exact reading skill involved in particular activities. If they find this difficult look at the activity pages together and talk about what you are being asked to do.

Talk about their answers to the third set of questions. Encourage your child to show you the activity they enjoyed most as well as the one they think they did best.

Look together at the activities which your child found hard. See if you can help pinpoint the problem.

HOW *you* CAN HELP

● If your child made mistakes on page 23, or found some activities hard, don't worry. It's important that they understand what they are doing, and you can help by *talking activities through* with them.

● Look for situations around the home where they can try out the different *reading skills*. For example, you can ask them to follow the directions on food labels, find out what time a certain programme is on television, or look for something in the small ads. ● If there are activities which your child particularly *enjoyed* try to take time to think of others like them. For example, if they enjoyed playing Tricia's Holiday Game, you could play other games with rules or invent your own games. ● All the skills in this book are those we use in *everyday life*, so involve your child in sharing them with you.

You don't have to be an expert to make a Success!